MW00943123

Grandma Marilyn's Wisdom

Taming a Know-It-All Taming Your Body

Marilyn Wightman

To order additional copies, please contact us.
BookSurge
www.booksurge.com
1-866-308-6235
orders@booksurge.com

CONTENTS

Introduction: My book is a labor of love. My words come straight from the heart and are from an 82 year young woman with a little wisdom, observation, common sense, heartfelt feelings for others and sensitivity for the happiness of others. Webster's definition of wisdom: "Challenges what has become accepted."

As I try to analyze the word wisdom, these are my thoughts. Wisdom can come to us at any age. At twenty, we feel much smarter than we did when we were eighteen when we thought we knew absolutely everything. Remember those days? I do. The thirties bring wisdom, as do the forties, fifties and sixties. When we reach eighty we may feel we have enough wisdom to write a book and share that wisdom with others. If I live to be one hundred, maybe I will write another book. But for now, this is my wisdom that I would like to share with you. After reading maybe the words will help you change some things in your life that have been accepted, though may need a change.

The main purpose of my book is to offer insightful answers to questions that many of us will agree are common concerns. It is meant to be positive, not negative. Hopefully there will be inspiration for adults and children alike. My hope is that it will bring more peace and calm in your relationships. May the words nudge you to take a step forward and to challenge accepted procedures in your life to see if a change is possible. The suggestions and ideas do make common sense but can be difficult to achieve; however, I have faith in people and I know anything is achievable if the desire is there.

You will also find suggestions on taking care of your body. These will include finding your will power, taking the word diet out of your vocabulary, relaxing, stretching, patience and more. If one is diligent, these habits are achievable and so worth every effort put forth.

Please read the words with an open mind so that you may help yourself and help others. I believe it can be an individual effort and a team effort. Please do not be timid but act in a determined manner.

Now may I tickle your fancy or stir your imagination to bring new ideas into your life as you start the first chapter of my book? I hope so. Enjoy!

Chapter 1
Growing In Wisdom

I believe it is important to know a little about a person who would wish to share her thoughts and wisdom on everyday life, so may I please introduce myself to you?

My name is Marilyn Wightman and my home is Ft. Myers, Florida. I am an 82 year young woman with a little wisdom that I would like to share with you. I was the youngest of three, having a sister and a brother. My sister was homecoming queen at Drake University in Des Moines, Iowa in the mid thirties. The Drake Relays game that night was broadcast by President Ronald Reagan during his sports broadcasting days. It was a very special occasion and very impressive for a 10 year old little girl. There was a parade in downtown Des Moines with my sister, Elaine, in an open convertible. This was, for sure, an unforgettable moment for me.

I have lived in 9 states and 16 cities. Des Moines, Cedar Rapids and Waterloo, Iowa; Annapolis, Maryland; Quantico, Virginia; Camp Lejeune, North Carolina; Sioux Falls, Huron and Rapid City, South Dakota; St. Paul, Minnesota; Omaha, Nebraska; Capistrano Beach, San Clemente and Dana Point, California; Cape Coral and Ft. Myers, Florida.

I fell in love at the age of 18. My soon to be husband, Bob, was 23. He was attending his last year at The United States Naval Academy in Annapolis, Maryland and was from my home town, Des Moines, Iowa. Bob's father was an Attorney in Des Moines with many attorneys in his firm. In his earlier years he was a Judge.

We met in the winter of 1944. It wasn't long before we were planning a wedding upon Bob's graduation in June of 1945. June of 1945 came and Bob found out he had not passed one of his subjects, and had to take another year. We did not want to wait another year to become husband and wife, so we decided to get married in secret while he finished another year. This was absolutely forbidden! Do you think we took a chance? You bet! But it worked.

We were married in October of 1945. My brother, Dick, was in the Army and stationed at Ft. Belvoir, Virginia. He and his wife, Yvonne, were by our side for the marriage. You might say these were exciting times! I lived in Annapolis and was fortunate to have a job as a secretary for an attorney from October until June. We were married a second time on June 5, 1946. This had to be done for the records.

Bob's greatest wish was to be accepted into the United States Marine Corps upon graduation from the Academy. This was difficult because only a few had this opportunity. Would you believe he actually drew a lucky number out of a hat to be able to become a 1st Lt. in the United States Marine Corps. The few others who became a Marine were able to do so having been a Marine upon receiving their appointment to the Academy. Bob was very happy to be a Marine, but did not want to have a career in the Marine Corps. His men had the utmost respect for him, as he did for them. While on maneuvers, he would dig in and do the same work as his men. Later we received many gifts from them as a way of showing their respect. Upon serving the required 3 years, Bob was honorably discharged in 1949.

While still in the Marine Corps we had two sons exactly 18 months apart. Patrick was born in July of 1947 in Des Moines, Iowa. Timothy was born in January of 1949 at the Marine Base in Camp Lejeune, North Carolina. We were a very happy family. Upon Bob's discharge, he took a job with Northwestern Bell Telephone Company in Cedar Rapids, Iowa. We moved to Cedar Rapids, bought our first home and Bob began his career.

It was now 1951, during the Korean War, and Bob was called back in for a year. He was stationed at Camp Pendleton, California. The family moved to California and we lived in Capistrano Beach. During that year Bob would volunteer many times to be sent to Korea. However, because he had a family, they would not let him go. We returned to Cedar Rapids in the spring of 1952.

A really wonderful and "once in a lifetime" opportunity came to us in 1953 when our sons were 4½ and 6. My husband's uncle was West Coast Editor of Look Magazine. We were offered a one week all expense paid trip to California. We would be featured in Look Magazine a few months later showing how wonderful a vacation can be in sunny California in the wintertime. We were thrilled and excited to say the least!

We traveled by train to California. We were treated quite wonderfully during our trip and many pictures were taken on the train. It was a night journey and the boys had bunk beds. They were thrilled!

Upon our arrival in Los Angeles, we were greeted by our story writer and photographer. We were then driven to the (still famous) Chateau Marmont Hotel. We checked in and went immediately to our room. We walked in and were surprised to find a beautiful suite. We were in awe of it all! We were also given a brand new red Chevrolet Convertible to use during our stay. We were happy campers, for sure!

The next day Bob's uncle took us to the MGM Commissary lunch room. This was indeed a very special day. While having lunch, Bob's uncle pointed to a beautiful blonde woman two tables over standing by a high chair. He asked us to "take a look" at her and said that her name was Marilyn Monroe. He then asked us to remember her name and said "she will become very famous and very soon." He was right! There were other famous stars in the lunchroom and we were goggle-eyed to say the least. We felt we shouldn't stare at everyone and Uncle Gene said, "Yes stare, they love it!"

The following day we headed south from Los Angeles on our way to La Jolla, San Diego and Palm Springs with many stops and lots of picture taking along the way. We followed the writer and photographer in their car on our journey. The boys were thrilled with our convertible and in case you were wondering, we did have the top down! I imagine more than one hundred pictures were taken.

Look Magazine came out a few months later and we were featured with a six page spread. Later we received a package with at least sixty 8x10 glossy photos. A photo album was made and has been enjoyed throughout the years. Great memories for sure and quite amazing, I must say.

It was now in the early fifties and we wished for more children. It was almost seven years after Timothy's birth before we had our third child. In September of 1955 we were blessed with another son and we named him Michael. He was born in Sioux Falls, South Dakota. In April of 1959, just three and a half years later, we were blessed with our fourth son, Jeffrey. He was born in Rapid City, South Dakota.

We were happy with our four boys and Patrick was nearly 15 years old. We were also thinking how wonderful it might be to add a daughter to our family. On cue and three and a half years later, in September of 1962, I was expecting our fifth child. Are you ready for this? You are exactly right—we had a girl! WOW, we were all in disbelief. Was she spoiled? Of course not! Well, maybe just a little. We named our little girl Susan. She was born in Omaha, Nebraska. There are many who have experienced this special event and can relate to this story.

We were now living in Omaha after moving from Cedar Rapids and Waterloo, Iowa, Sioux Falls, Huron and Rapid City, South Dakota and Saint Paul, Minnesota. All was great with our lives. My husband was doing well with his career and was now General Plant Manager of the State of Nebraska.

Three years later, in 1965, my husband told me he had noticed a lump in his neck that had been there for about a year. I immediately made an appointment with the doctor. We had very devastating news. The lump was malignant and he would need to go through chemotherapy. At the same time, I found out that I was pregnant with our 6th child. I thought this is not the best time to have another child, but you need to accept life and we did what we needed to do.

Bob was so brave and went through chemotherapy through the winter while still working and we were sure he would recover. Through the winter months the cancer grew and it was now in his lungs and throughout his body. Bob originally kept the lump a secret for a year. You can see how important it is to seek help immediately when you suspect you might have a problem?

It was now May, 1966, and I had just given birth to our 6th child. And yes, just a little over three and a half years after our daughter was born. Our 6th child was a boy and we named him Jon. Jon was born in Omaha, Nebraska. When Jon was 10 days old, I had a gut feeling that the Mayo Clinic would have some answers for us. I chartered a plane and took my husband to Rochester, Minnesota on June 5, 1966. My mother came from California to be with me for the trip. The news was not good. We were given the news you don't want to hear. Bob had three months to live. We were in shock and didn't really know how we would get through the next three months. One thing I knew for sure was that during his remaining months, I would take care of my husband at home, no matter what!

Our oldest son, Patrick, was in the Marine Corps and stationed at Camp Pendleton, California going through Boot Camp. Our baby was only 2 weeks old. What were we to do? We had many dear friends who offered their help. One friend counseled me with some great words of wisdom saying that many would offer their help to me and when they did, I should absolutely accept that help. He told me I would do the same for them. With that wonderful advice, we sent our two middle sons, Michael and Jeffrey, to be with some dear friends in Rapid City, South Dakota for the summer. My second son, Tim, stayed at home.

He was 17 and in High School. I really do not know how I could have possibly been strong through it all without his arm and presence to uphold me. My husband's parents kept our daughter, Susan, in their home in Des Moines, Iowa. They would bring her to us on weekends. I kept our baby at home, so that he could see his father and his father could see him.

The family had planned a 50th wedding anniversary for my mom and dad at our home in Omaha on July 1st. I was certainly going to cancel the get together, but my husband—bless his dear heart—insisted that everyone come, and they did. My brother and his wife and their four children, plus my mom and dad, drove to Omaha from Portland, Oregon. It was a great reunion and Bob was his usual brave self and, though in pain, did enjoy the event.

My husband passed away on September 8, 1966 in the middle of the night as I lay beside him. He was 44 years old. As I write these words it all seems so unreal and that it didn't really happen, but it did. Oh so sad! We had a wonderful life, healthy children and all of a sudden there was a stop to it all. But you must go on and be thankful for all of the good you still have in your life. In the days that followed, I kept thinking to myself that there would be an end to cancer soon, but not soon enough for my husband. That was 43 years ago. Treatment has advanced, but it is still important to go to the doctor as soon as you suspect something. If you do, go immediately!

My husband's death left me with six children. Our oldest son was now in Vietnam and our youngest was four months old. It was a tremendously sad and difficult time; however, I am a survivor. I must say, my children were my salvation!

Eventually I remarried. His name was Dan and he had just lost his wife to cancer. He had also been through some very sad times and we could certainly relate to one another. Two lovely daughters were added to my six children. Their names are Jan and Jill. He was a good man and we had a good life together. Sadly, the marriage ended after 16 years. Any marriage with a family is a challenge, and a step-father/step-mother situation is especially difficult.

When my children were small, I was fortunate to be a stay at home mom. Later, when Jon was still at home, I did have several jobs from a Housekeeper for condos at Ft. Myers Beach, 3 plus years of Marketing Research, working for the Census Bureau and Real Estate in California and Florida. I enjoyed my working days.

At present, I have been happily married for 19 years to a wonderful man whose name is Joe. We met in November of 1989 in San Clemente, California. We were married in December of 1990. I was in Real Estate at the time with my son Tim, and his wife Jeanette. Joe and I have been married for 19 years. I have 5 sons and a daughter and Joe has 5 sons and a daughter. Can you imagine the odds of each of us having a daughter and five sons? We still talk about the uniqueness of it all! His children's names are Cheryl, Ned and Neal who are twins, Tony, Bret and Joe. Between us, we have 28 grandchildren and 7 great grandchildren. Soon, we will have 29 grandchildren and 9 great grandchildren. We are blessed for sure.

There was an additional sadness in our family when I lost my oldest son, Patrick, in 1994. He was born in 1947 and he was 47 when he passed away. As I said before, I am a survivor. You have to be.

Yes indeed, I have many people in my life. It is a special feeling for me to have so many family members and we have many family reunions. One very special reunion was when we all celebrated my 80th birthday. My children play the guitar and write songs. Michael wrote a beautiful song for his mom for the occasion. Title: Mother. I love my birthday. It is New Year's Day!

Through these many years, I have had the opportunity to see five Presidents in person. President Roosevelt in Des Moines, Iowa; President Gerald Ford on a golf course in California; President Ronald Wilson Reagan in Cape Coral, Florida; President George Herbert Walker Bush and his wife, Barbara and President George Walker Bush on the golf course in Boca Grande, Florida on December 27, 2000. That was very special for me.

This challenging and varied life I have led is my wisdom.

Chapter 2
Taming a Know-It-All

Hello. Welcome to my thoughts about a Know-it-All, and other bits of wisdom. I do hope you will enjoy the read and find its importance in your life. Hopefully you will glean some mind provoking ideas that will be helpful to you and yours.

Looking back on my life, I realize that my awareness of simple everyday conversations did not historically grab me as they do today. Being in tune with another's feelings is extremely important in order to have meaningful and pleasant relationships. We often forget how important these precious human needs are in our daily communications with another person. The saying "Think before you speak," has true meaning. This true meaning can be difficult for all of us to achieve. You **can** think before you speak, but do you?

I'll get right to the point. First of all, what is a know-it-all? Webster defines one this way: "Pretending or proclaiming to know much about almost everything."

Classic example of a know-it-all: A news item or an event is offered to the know-it-all. The response is usually: "I know." Or it may be: "Yah, I know." A better answer might be "Really?" or "Thanks for sharing."

This is where you "think before you speak." Even though you already know what was offered, why not be thoughtful and give the second answer. Repeated answers like the first one leads the questioner to give up trying to tell the know-it-all anything, because he already knows the answer he will receive.

Another example of a know-it-all is one who interrupts a conversation with their thoughts, as if their thoughts and ideas are the best. They are not patient with the other one and would like to have the last word. They seem to **flaunt** their authority or intelligence. I believe we can all be guilty of this practice at one time or another. This does not include an intellectual exchange of ideas. In many of these conversations, both are right about a certain subject and each have a different take on the subject. Neither is a know-it-all, only sharing an opinion; however, there are others that just need to have the last word on a certain subject. You know them and so do I.

Are you a know-it-all? Is there anything you can do about it? Do you wish to do anything about it? Do you care? Do you believe people may be talking about you being a know-it-all behind your back? Do you honestly believe you know it all? These are questions to ponder and questions only you can answer.

My observation is that many people are know-it-alls. When I question a friend or family member if they know a know-it-all, the response is almost 100% "yes" or "I am one myself." Don't you think this is quite interesting? How would you answer this question?

Many people are avid readers and have a degree or two and are extremely intelligent. I say kudos to them! I believe it is human nature to want to have that smart and aware feeling. However, try not to make the other one feel unimportant and unaware. Try to let them share the feeling of having something to bring to the table. It will make you feel good. You may know a lot, but don't be a know-it-all. There is a difference. My humble suggestion is to **not** be a know-it-all while talking with others and be humble and kind and think before you speak. Others will appreciate how you are coming across. Your **response** when someone gives you news of the day, or whatever, is important. News of the day or an item in the paper does not always need a response of "I know" or "I've already seen it." Those who constantly receive this answer are left feeling deflated and unimportant and often don't wish to communicate with one who cannot think before he speaks. I can attest to this and I would bet that many who are reading these words can also relate. Why not say: "Really?" Or you could say "Really, I believe I heard that—thanks for sharing." I know that many arguments and quarrels can take place from this behavior. In my opinion, acting with a kind response takes away the title of know-it-all to a kind and gentle person who thinks before he speaks. It is as simple as that. Or is it? Actually, it is very difficult to change this habit. Try it and you will find out how difficult it can be.

From my observations, there seem to be many people who fit the category of a know-it-all. And don't you just love a know-it-all? Maybe you are one and don't even realize it. Bet one thing—you may be one but have never given it a thought. After all, it is always the other guy—right? Do you have negative feelings towards a know-it-all? Bet you do. Do you relate to friends and family that another person you both know is a know-it-all? Sometimes it isn't fun to be around them but you hold your thoughts and bite your tongue and somehow get through it. One observation I have made is that this person could be a family member or friend who, except for this one bug-a-boo, is the greatest person you have ever known. Guess you just accept it because you may also be a know-it-all. Wow! Now that's a scary thought. I may also be a know-it-all? As I put words to paper, I wonder if others are bothered by this one characteristic in others. I believe the answer is a big YES.

As I ponder these thoughts I must say that knowing it all, or knowing much about many subjects, is wonderful. I have family members and friends who know a lot but keep it to themselves as often as possible. They seem to know enough not to **flaunt** it and want to be the humble one and take the back seat. This is difficult to do if you are not of that personality.

Do you know the true meaning of humble? Humble—a pleasant and meaningful word that evokes a trait you may wish to embrace. Being humble shows a consciousness of one's own defects or short-comings; not proud, modest, not arrogant or assertive. Do you believe you are able to be a humble person? Can you take a back seat? Can you give the glory to others and be happy about it and swallow your pride? It is definitely a learning experience. Some will learn and accept and some will not.

Arguments can often start between husband and wife, siblings, friends, co-workers, family members in general (including children) and partners because of one who thinks he knows everything. Try **not** to let this happen in **your** life. Be the one who thinks of another's feelings because they do have them, you know, and think before you speak. Be gentle when you respond to another. Try to bite your tongue before saying something suddenly and with little thought. Have tact and show kindness, courtesy and compassion for others. Your heart will feel good if you let the other one feel important because of **your** goodness. Try it. You just may like it. I have tried it and it does make the heart feel good.

There are often daily arguments and quarrels with this behavior among couples and it isn't any fun at all. It is not easy to change old habits. I very often stumble and catch myself speaking before I think. Many of us do; however, if one day at a time or one time a week it is successful, at least it is a start. If husband and wife can communicate this problem together, it is very helpful. Read "The Rainbow Story" at the end of this chapter. My husband and I practice quite often. When he catches himself and thinks first it is such a total joy—you cannot believe! This also happens with me in my responses to him. It seems like such a little thing, but in the whole of things, it is a huge accomplishment. Little things **do** mean a lot. I might add here that older siblings can reap huge benefits if they learn to practice this while they are young.

When a disagreement is an issue between husband and wife, or partners, one solution that can help solve this disagreement is to write a note or a letter to the other. It can help save the arguments that occur back and forth that often end up with no solution at all. While writing, always acknowledge the other side of the story. This way, you can state your views and ask for their views. When writing a note or a letter, there are no interruptions. They can then answer with a note or letter of their own. It truly is a good solution to many problems. Try it. I have, and it works every time.

I have attempted to relate what I believe is important for good relationships between all of us. You now have suggestions on how to start that journey to achieve that goal. It is a very difficult journey, believe me. If this reading seems trivial to you, then just maybe you are the one who needs to heed the words you are reading. If you are one who doesn't understand or who has frequent arguments, disagreements and quarrels, then maybe you are a know-it-all.

If each of us would try to take the back seat just some of the time (it is too crowded in front) and not take the frosting from the other's cake, there would be more peace and calm. This could mean freedom from disagreement and quarrels. Then, just maybe, we may live longer.

Following, you will read some true family stories relating to these problems that do have an answer, though very difficult to achieve. It is all in the scheme of things; a plan or program of action. I do not have a degree in psychology, nor am I a college graduate. My words and thoughts are from an 82 year young woman with a little wisdom, **observation** and common sense. If you like what you have read so far hang on, we are just getting started.

Chapter 3
True Family Stories

My Son's Awareness

All of my children have encouraged me with my book. As I have shared my thoughts with them, they have supported me and given me some guidance. They felt my words would reach many and that my words were needed.

One day I received an email from my son, Jeff. As I read it, I was full of joy. My words were now reaching my own family and Jeff wished to share his story with his mom. He stated that he had been a little too forward at work one day and had interrupted a co-worker so he could say what he had to say. Having three years seniority on the co-worker, he felt he knew so much more. But then he realized how he was coming across. He apologized to the co-worker and let him finish what he started to say. As he listened, he realized the co-worker really did have something to say. He also realized how he can often be too forward. It made him take a good look at himself. I guess my words are helping my own son and my wish is that they will help others. This is the purpose of my book.

My son thought I was writing the book for my kids, but then he realized that everyone needs help in this area of their lives. He related to me that he also remembers (as my daughter did) when I would walk out of the room while he was talking. Now he knows why. He said he is really going to work on it. I am proud of him, to know that he can admit these personal feelings to his mom. If this book can help my own children then, just maybe, it may help others.

My Daughter's Awareness

My words were also touching my own daughter, Susan, as well as Jeff. I would like to share our story with you.

Susan had a project doing some painting in her daughter's home. She asked if I would like to join her. We were discussing my book in the making. I gently approached the subject of a know-it-all. She related to me that she actually felt she was one. As we pursued the conversation, I felt comfortable to tell her about some past episodes. As I continued with some examples, she said; "I always wondered why you would be turned off at times and walk away from a conversation." She always wondered if she had done or said something that wasn't to my liking. She wondered why I wouldn't tell her. Guess the answer to that is that I didn't want an argument to pursue and felt she may not understand. I was also trying to avoid a confrontation that would lead to nowhere.

We were so thankful this misunderstanding of the past was coming to a close. She tried hard that day not to be a know-it-all and I was so proud of her! At one point, she said; "now, just there, I thought before I spoke." She was now aware and it made her very happy. And it made her mom very happy! Too bad we weren't able to settle this problem long ago. Try not to let it take that long for you.

My Own Awareness

I have been trying hard to practice what I preach. What's good for the goose is good for the gander. My son Jon called me late one afternoon to let me know my favorite movie would be on that night. I asked him the time and the channel. I opted not to tell him that I already knew it was on and that I had a note by my chair to remind me. Instead, I thanked him so much for letting me know. A true know-it-all would have for sure, answered "yah, I know." I was happy with myself and felt I practiced the right thing by following my own advice "think before you speak." Remember your **response** is key here. Can you imagine how he might have felt if he had called me for nothing? He might have felt that way if I had answered "yah, I know." I know how happy he was to give his mom this information and wanted him to know

I appreciated his call. Now when he reads this, he will chuckle and appreciate the story. It **is** the little things that count.

My response to him was the exact response he would give to another. He is a great responder, as is my son Michael. Remember, it is the little things that count!

My Husband's Awareness

A few years ago my husband and I were on our way home from Naples, Florida, after attending a Greg Norman Golf Tournament. During our ride, I spotted a very tall and beautiful white building with a unique design. I thought to myself that I would like my husband to see this building. As the traffic slowed down I said "look over there at that beautiful white building." He looked and said "Yah, I've seen it." I was surprised. Had he seen it? If so, maybe another answer could have been "yes that is beautiful, I believe I saw a story about it in the paper." Oh how happy I would have been.

My thinking, though I agree was petty, was this. Of all the buildings we had passed, how did he know in an instant that he had seen that particular building? And you know, he probably had seen the building. He is an avid reader and may have seen an article about the building in the paper. I must tell you the rest of the 45 minute ride home was a quiet ride because I was bothered by his response.

I could question myself as to why that should have bothered me. It was such a stupid little thing, or was it? Often, I feel more at fault (if it is a fault) than the episode itself. Why do I care and should I care? I can also say that many of us have both of these characteristics. Many arguments and sad and unhappy feelings can result in these behaviors. I believe that in life it is the little things that count in our relationships and that we can all work on these little things 24/7. Can you? Many of us are guilty of this behavior. I often catch myself saying, "I've seen it" or something similar. If you have seen it, at least add that it is beautiful. It is very difficult to catch yourself before you speak. Try it and you will find out just how difficult it can be.

Since this episode happened a few months ago, my husband has been a dear. I can tell by his responses, that he thinks before he speaks. I praise him highly for being able to understand and practice what his wife's book is all about! I must say, I have also improved. My book seems to be helping both of us and my wish is that it will help you. Little things do mean a lot.

Books-a-Million

While browsing in Books-A-Million one day, I searched the self help section for any title that might suggest a know-it-all. Previously, I had looked in libraries for a similar book and found nothing. I wanted to know how many books had already been written on the subject, before I put my thoughts on paper. I found nothing and the section was long. I went to the front desk to seek assistance. I asked the young lady at the computer if she could search for a title "Know-it-All." She found nothing. She decided to look for different titles that may suggest a Know-it-All. Nothing came up. I then asked her a question. "Do you know what a know-it-all is?" She answered -"I sure do, I just broke up with my boyfriend because he was one." She went on to explain some situations. She said that no matter what she would tell him or say to him, he always already knew it. She said it made her feel unimportant and that she knew nothing. Then she added – "who needs that in their life?" I shared with the young lady that I was writing a book about know-it-alls and asked her if I could share her story. She said "You sure can."

The Rainbow Story

Would you like to follow the rainbow on a journey to a pot of gold? The gold could be a medal in a competition or the effort of two parties acting independently and together to find a common ground with each other. Both could be winners if the desire and challenge is there. Here are some suggestions for the journey. The suggestions are for the receiver of negative responses that just may help **both** parties. Offer this to your negative responder, be it husband, wife, friend, family member or co-worker. Have a conversation that can gently lead to the following question. When you always respond with "Yah, I know" or "I've already seen it," I would like to tell you how it makes me feel. Is that okay with you? First, I know I often give the same response to you. When I **receive** this response from you however, I feel sad, frustrated, unimportant and discouraged. All of this is because I feel a need for respect, appreciation, connection and importance. I feel I cannot offer anything new to you because you will answer with "I know." You may feel the same way with my responses. I would suggest to both of us that our responses be more positive towards each other. I believe if we both try hard, it would be a step in the right direction. Then, just maybe, there would be more peace and harmony between us on a daily basis. Shall we try it together and see what happens? It won't be easy and it won't always be accomplished, but if we try real hard, I just know there can be an improvement. Let's try it, we just may like it!

Please note that The Rainbow Story can also be done in writing as I offered earlier. For some, this is an easier path.

Chapter 4
Helpful Thoughts for a Know-It-All

Remove your egos—give them away. This is one of the most challenging things you may ever do, be it friend to friend, spouse to spouse, co-workers, partners or siblings. Who will be the brave one? It is best to share the responsibility. Try the Rainbow Story. What have you got to lose? Nothing! What have you got to gain? The love, appreciation, admiration and grace of others! Just bite the bullet, bite your tongue and go for it! Don't be a "one-upper" unless you want to be. Do you want to be a "one-upper?" Do you want people to talk about you behind your back? If you are willing to swallow your pride, I promise it won't choke you. Be humble. Don't take the frosting from the other's cake. Think before you speak. We can all try this. Your friend or family member would love to be able to share something new, special and exciting without receiving the answer "Yah, I know," or "I've seen it." Sound familiar? I'm sure it does. Is it a small and trivial thing that one should ignore? I don't believe so. It can hurt relationships. Remember the gal in Books-A-Million? Your response is key here. Think before you speak and be compassionate. Reserve the glory for others while having conversations. It's the little things that count. Spouses have many arguments in this area which could be avoided with some good hard dedication and a little humility on both sides. Work on it together and share the responsibility. If both are willing, it could be very helpful and, in fact, vital. Could the constant bickering and arguing end in divorce or years of an unhappy life together? The answer to that question is a big YES. Try not to clutter your lives with unnecessary spats. Life is too short. Try to be dedicated to this frequent and nagging problem. Patience is a virtue. Try to be the patient one.

If you are not an annoying know-it-all and are zapped with an annoying know-it-all, don't always feel upset. Let it go. You also need to practice not always being bothered. If you can see that the other person is trying, give them credit. You may not be perfect at this game either. Think about it. Please remember these words and try to do your part in having a more calm and peaceful life. I guarantee you will be happier!

Chapter 5
Taming Your Body
Finding Your Will
power

It has been said there is nothing new under the sun. There are only new perspectives that have already been thought of by many. There are a zillion (maybe an exaggeration) ideas, suggestions, techniques, sure things and absolutes for the care and healthy maintenance of your body. I would like to share my perspectives on the care and maintenance of the body.

Many years ago, when I was in my early thirties and we had three young sons, I had started to diligently pursue my exercise programs. I will share some conversations that I had with friends seeking ways to take care of their bodies. Hopefully these words I share with you will help you on your path of taking care of your wonderful body. As I was pursuing this challenge in my life, my friends would ask me for some advice on how to accept this challenge – and it definitely is a challenge. We were all young and had 3 or 4 children at home.

I would share my program with them and their answer would be; "I don't have time." Does this sound familiar? Have you given this answer to others, and to yourself, that you don't have time? It may be true that you don't have time, **or** could it be that you just don't want to do it. I believe it should be a priority to take care of your body. Probably one of the biggest challenges you may have in your life. I was fortunate to be a stay at home mom. However, I understand how difficult it must be for men and women alike, to find time to take care of their bodies, during their working years. But I do believe it is a must! Just ten or fifteen minutes while watching television can do wonders for your body and for you. Later in this chapter you will read ideas on how to discover your will power. You will need this will power for taking care of your body and for many things in life. Taking care of your body does not need to be a 24/7 commitment. However, it should be a lifetime commitment. This means you will not always be able to exercise. There may be weeks or even months or a year or more where you are not able to pursue this challenge. That's OK, just get back to it as soon as possible and make it a lifetime commitment. You will love yourself.

Finding Your Will Power

We had just moved to St. Paul, Minnesota and our fourth son, Jeff, was three months old. I was

32 years of age and maintaining my weight quite well, but had gained 6 or 8 pounds. At that time I was aware that it is easier to lose a small amount of weight, rather than 20 to 80 pounds. My observation had been that many women my age and with a child or two tended to gain a lot of weight. I had more than one friend who had fallen into this category. I thought this was sad. I felt a diet would be okay, but that it would be too easy to fall off that diet. I would be on an up and down roller coaster through the years. My decision was to take the word "diet" out of my vocabulary. What would I do? What would I do? After contemplating for many days, I thought of a plan.

We were entertaining some friends one evening and I decided I would not eat one bite of food that night. Maybe this would get me on my way to honest will power, self control and discipline and would really spur me on for the days, weeks, months and years to follow. My plan sounded easy enough, but actually was quite difficult. It turned out to be one of the best decisions I have made in my life. One thing I did know for sure was that I did not want to put on that extra 20 to 80 pounds in the next several years!

Our get together with our friends was not dinner. I had prepared various snacks including deviled eggs, chips and dips, sandwich meat, cheese spreads and more. I also made a cake. The evening went well and I was following my plan and becoming very proud of myself. Our friends left and my husband had gone to bed. I was alone in the kitchen cleaning up and there were bits of leftovers. Some I tossed and others I covered for the refrigerator. With each bit of food I thought I would just take a taste—just a taste—just a taste, but I didn't. I was really proud of myself at this point, and then the cake appeared. It looked so good! As I eyed it, I noticed a cutting knife on the side of the platter. I picked up the knife and said to myself, "I will just swipe my finger on this tiny bit of frosting and have a taste." I had been so good and this surely wouldn't hurt. "Wouldn't hurt who?" I thought. It would hurt me and all I had achieved during the evening. Do you think I gave in at this point? Absolutely not! I went to bed feeling I had followed my plan and I was very happy!

When morning came, I cannot begin to tell you how proud I was for achieving the will power I was looking for these many years. You might say this was the beginning of finding my will power and self control victory for the rest of my life. This event has stayed with me throughout the years with the satisfaction of knowing I did it! You can too. My suggestion to those who would like to feel proud of themselves in this area of their life is this: JUST DO IT!! It worked for me and it can work for you. You may have another plan that will work for you. If so, use it to find **your** will power. I have told this story many times and my granddaughters love it. They are proud with the success they have had maintaining their weight.

Now that I had found my will power, I needed to select the right foods to sustain me through the years. Salads have always been a favorite of mine and there are many foods you can add to a salad. Fruit salads are also good. Of course there are veggies you can add and seafood. Whenever we go out to dinner, I will always be able to pick a salad from many selections. There are also times I order a steak and baked potato. If you are diligent during the week, it is ok to splurge on weekends. It makes it all worth while. Save the weekends for that pie ala mode or chocolate malt. You will have a favorite that you can look forward to on the weekend. Try to stay away from the chips, fattening foods and candy. Save those candy bars for the weekend. You know what they can do to your body, if you over indulge. You will discover many great foods that will sustain you and keep you healthy. I have found that chewing gum helps the urge to eat something that you really don't need. You can do it, but you will need will power and self control.

Stretching

You can ride in a stretch limo, stretch a rubber band, wear stretch jeans and you can stretch the truth; however, the best stretch is to stretch your body. Your body will love you!

I am sure you already know that stretching is good for you. As we age, it becomes more difficult to reach high above your head or to stoop down for an item on the lowest shelf in the grocery store or to be agile like you were when you were young. Believe it or not, it **is** possible! I have a few tips that may be helpful.

During our younger years, we are usually quite active and do a lot of normal stretching. Because I have consistently stretched throughout the years, I am able to stand straight and bend down and touch the palms of my hands to the floor with my legs straight. I am also able to sit down and touch my head to the floor with my legs apart. Through the years I have done stretching exercises on a regular basis. I do miss some weeks, but this has been a way of life and part of the way I take care of my body. Your body will love you for the care you give it. Anyone can do this if they have stretching as part of their "keeping fit" regime. It is quite nice to be able to reach high, and bend down easily and get up again, especially when you reach the age of eighty. My grandchildren are amazed when I touch my palms to the floor. They are not able to do this. If they had stretching as a part of their fitness regime, they could do it easily. It just takes dedication, patience and a "lifetime commitment" of taking care of your wonderful body!

There are many programs for stretching that are great. You will find them on the internet, TV, and in the newspaper and most of them will work. My system tends to be quite simple and may not be as thorough as some, but it works for me and it can work for you. I was advised long ago that it is better to keep it simple and consistent. Your program shouldn't be so intense that you are tempted to give up. Setting it aside for a short time is OK if you remain relatively consistent in the long run at staying with your "keeping fit" regime. There will be times when you will need to give it up for a few months or more. Just get back to it as soon as you can. Remember, this is a "lifetime commitment."

Always limber up before you stretch. You can do this with a fast five minute walk, or you can do a little pre-stretching and bending. You will have your favorite way of limbering up. The following is how I do my stretching.

1. Sit on the floor with legs together and straight in front of you.
2. Bend the right leg and bring your right foot to your left knee.
3. Slowly bring your hands down and touch your left toes.
4. Keep this position for 2 or 3 seconds and **only** till you feel the strain.
5. Repeat with the left leg – bending and bringing your left foot to your right leg.
6 Start this program 2 or 3 times a week and work your way up to 5 times per week. In time, you will be good with only three times per week, because your body will be limber.
7 Try to make your goal of 30 bend downs on each side.

If this is your first time, you may be able to only reach your shin with your hands. That's OK! In time you will be able to go all the way. And in time, you will be able to put that foot to your knee or thigh. Practice this 2 or 3 times a week at first and then try 3 to 5 times per week. Soon you will be good with only three times per week, because your body will be limber. When you are limber you will also be able to sit on the floor, with legs apart, and bend down and touch your head to the floor. Try to make this your goal for your lifetime commitment of taking care of your wonderful body. Remember, if you miss weeks or months or a year, that's ok. Just get back to it when you are able. When I miss some weeks or months, my body gets very stiff. Makes you realize the good it is doing. This stretching exercise is also fun to do in the bathtub. By the way, I can still do this stretching exercise.

When you have achieved this stretching exercise and your body is limber, try this. Stand tall and with your legs **straight**, bend down and touch the floor with you hands. In time, you will be able to touch the palms of your hands to the floor. The body loves to be stretched and it is amazing how wonderful it is to be agile as you reach those senior years.

Another stretching exercise I like is to stand tall and clasp your hands behind your head. With your shoulders back (don't slouch) slowly twist your upper body only from side to side. Stop for a moment with each turn. Your lower body must remain firm and not move. Start with ten or twenty and work your way up to 100 turns. You can also bend from your right side to your left side in this same position, remembering to stop for a moment at each turn. With this stretching exercise, it is helpful if you are able to stand in front of a mirror to check yourself and to make sure that your lower body does not move. Try to work your way up to 100 bends. If you want an hour glass figure, especially ladies, this stretch will help you get there. Consistency is vital here. You can start with two or three times per week. Always remember that if you miss days, weeks or months, that is ok. It can be another lifetime commitment and one that you will be able to do when you choose. Stretching will help you become limber. You can miss stretching for a period of time. When you do, you will find your body is not as agile. Just get back to it and your body will be agile once again.

Walking

Another great "keeping fit" exercise is walking. I believe walking is probably one of the best exercises you can do for your body. In my early forties, I decided to get serious about having a healthy life style and one I could truly keep. I was happy to achieve my will power with the food that one glorious night and was maintaining my weight. Through those years, my children thought I would actually look like a salad one day because

I ate so many. I felt it was now time to seriously start working on an exercise program that I would be able to maintain.

I began my new lifestyle with a two mile walk every morning. I was so proud of myself, but I would tell myself that I would need to do this for the rest of my life and that seemed like such a long time. It was a frightening thought; however, a thought you have to accept if you want to reach your goal. I walked for a few weeks and then decided I would ride my bike 2 miles each day for variety. This is another super exercise that is very pleasant and something you can do most every day. We lived in Florida so it wasn't a problem. Also, I was fortunate to be a stay at home mom. I would talk to myself and say "I can do this." Then I would say "No, I don't want to do this." For some reason (human nature I believe) it took a while for it to sink into my head. I realized this would be "for life" if I wanted to achieve the results I had set for myself. This was the hardest part for me, to actually talk myself into the fact that this is the way it would be. I knew I had to make up my mind that there would be exercise for my body of some kind if I wished to maintain a healthy body throughout my life. Thankfully, I made that decision and it has lasted through the years. I strongly believe the will power I found with the cake episode helped me with this decision.

My favorite exercise has been walking. This exercise is good for the heart and is an all over great exercise for the body. I chose to walk 20 minutes, usually 4 to 5 times per week. I walk very fast and people often ask me if I am going to a fire. Usually I will walk outdoors, but if it is chilly or raining, I walk inside. Those living in the cold winter states, as I did for many years, can walk inside. Just set your timer for 20 minutes and start walking from the kitchen to the bedrooms and back again. Walk fast! Have the television on as it helps pass the time. I will often carry a 5 pound weight in each hand and lift them above my head and up and down at my side as I walk. The KEY here is to be consistent. If you miss a week or 2 months or a year, it's okay. Just get back to it and all will not be lost. Remember a lifetime commitment and not 24/7. It seems easier when you think of it that way. You may want to walk 30 minutes each day. I had a friend who did the 30 minutes each day. She advised me to do the same. I tried it for a while but would find myself not liking it and actually not walking some days because 30 minutes seemed long for me. Silly I thought, but if I wanted to be consistent, I was better with my routine of 20 minutes. Better to do 20 minutes 4 or 5 times per week, than 30 minutes now and then. My husband had me beat in the walking department. You see, he was a Marathon runner. He did the New York Marathon and others. This is an extreme difference from my 20 minutes per day to his 15 to 25 miles per day!

There are many ways to exercise the body. I chose walking and stretching. I also belonged to fitness centers at different stages of my life, while at the same time, continued walking. My daughter loves walking, but also loves swimming. There are many ways to exercise your body. The bottom line is to exercise your body as a "keeping fit" regime throughout your life. If the exercise is interrupted for a short or long period of time, get right back to it. Whatever you decide, I'm rooting for you!

Just Relax

Has anyone ever told you to relax? I have realized through the years that relaxing can rid the body of tension headaches and a Charlie horse that grabs your leg in the middle of the night. These are just two of the many painful problems the body can experience. When you think about your wonderful body and how hard it works from sunrise to sunset and beyond, you have to wonder how this can be. Our body is truly amazing! Maybe, just maybe, your body needs a rest now and then and would like some help.

My awareness about relaxing came when I was in my late forties. I was having tension headaches in my neck, though nothing as severe as a migraine. Headaches are very uncomfortable. The advice given to me was to relax my body as often as I could. My husband would tell me to relax from my head to my toes. He could see that though I was trying, I still didn't get it! He would constantly remind me to relax my toes and other areas of my body. I thought I was accomplishing the job, but I wasn't. When I finally understood and learned to relax, my tension headaches went away and have never come back.

One needs to be aware of relaxing the body. You can actually relax while driving your car. You can relax while at the computer and while watching television. When you become aware of the benefits of relaxing, you will think of your own ways to relax. When my tension headaches went away, that was proof enough for me.

My mother was also a great advocate of relaxing. In restaurants, she would help someone who was choking. She would go to their table and get them to completely relax and the choking would stop. It sounds almost impossible to do, but you can relax when you really try; however, this would not be true with someone needing the Heim-lich maneuver.

Have you ever had a charley horse in your thigh or calf in the middle of the night? That is when it often happens. How painful it can be! I do have one once in a while. I bet you can guess what I do. I don't move, but I completely relax my whole body, especially the leg that is in pain, and let it go completely limp! It will really hurt for 20 or 30 seconds, but be patient and the pain will go away. You can feel that muscle move back into position. It has worked for me every time and it absolutely amazes me. Try it!

At times, while swallowing food or liquid that goes down the wrong way, you may start to cough to clear your throat. Many times the more you cough, the less the problem improves. You guessed it. Relax! You will have to really work to relax, but if you do, your throat will get the message and be thankful. While relaxing, you may need to cough a little, but keep relaxing. Every muscle that was tense will now be relaxed. This technique has always worked for me, though it took a lot of concentration before I mastered it. Try it.

When flying, I often have a problem with my ears plugging. If I can truly swallow, it helps so much. On my last flight, I tried something new. My swallowing wasn't working, so I relaxed my shoulders and bowed my head. I completely relaxed for a few minutes. The ears actually cleared quite a bit, but not all the way. It made me realize more than ever how helpful relaxing can be. I believe the body desperately needs you to relax any time you can. Remember, while driving your car, you can relax quite a bit and still be a safe driver. While sitting at the computer, you can actually relax. Notice if your toes are always tense. If they are, relax them. Your body will love you when you learn to relax!

Standing Straight

Years ago I remember my mother asking my sister and brother and I to stand straight. She would mainly impress this on my brother with a firm slap on the back. One day my brother's friend was over and my mother gave him a firm slap on his bare back. The friend didn't mind and accepted the advice with a smile. That was many years ago and I can still remember this boy. His name was Dexter. I guess when something impresses you, the memory stays with you.

This advice in my youth has stayed with me. My daughter is tall and when she was young I constantly reminded her to stand straight. After she married, I would send her notes to post around the house. She soon got the message. My son, Jeff, was also reminded to stand straight. He would always tell me that he did stand straight. Later, he related to me that while walking through an airport, he looked at himself in the windows and couldn't believe how his shoulders were slouched. From that point on, he decided to stand straight. You will not only look better, it is good for your body to stand straight.

Stomach In

Holding your stomach in can be difficult. It just seems easier to relax and let it go. Years ago I started holding my stomach in and it didn't take long before it became natural. A good motto is to stand straight and hold your stomach in. Some of the dress styles with over blouses seem to let one not care if their stomach protrudes. With this dress style, no one will see. The same goes for men's clothes. I believe it is not a good habit to get into. Try it and stick to it and before long it will become natural. Those with good posture look much better. Notice when you are shopping how much better those with good posture look, compared to those with poor posture.

Please know that these are only suggestions that may be helpful to some and not all.

Only You Can Take Care of You

This is true. We need to count on ourselves first and then hope to receive help along the way. As we are growing up, our parents help us every step of the way while teaching us to help ourselves. We learn many lessons through our journey into adulthood. There comes a time in our adult life to take control and follow our gut feelings and senses and to do the right thing in taking care of our body. We can and will ignore it for a period of time. There is always tomorrow, right? But while ignoring it, we can hear that voice in our head saying "When are you going to make that important decision? When are you going to realize that you and you alone need to make the decision to have will power and self-control in your life, the traits that will help you in all areas of your life?" These traits will help you take command of your body so it can be healthy. They can help you make important decisions. They can help you in your personal life. They can help you to be patient. They can help you to be understanding and appreciative. They can help you communicate with others in positive ways.

It happened to me and it can happen to you. It does not happen overnight, but rest assured that through the years you will achieve something that will make you proud. These traits have stayed with me through the years to my amazement, and I believe they are continuing to grow as I sit here and write my book.

Chapter 6
Gems for Thought

Listeners

Are you a good listener? Years ago my husband and I joined Amway. We went to a convention in Tampa, Florida. There were many hundreds in the audience. The first person on stage was a gentleman and he had one question for the audience. The question was this. "What is the greatest gift you can give to another person?" We were all mumbling different answers. Guess what the answer was? To listen! Many of us know those who do not listen. What is that catch phrase? "It's all about me." Try to listen when someone is sharing a story with you. I have a nephew, Dan, who is one of the greatest listeners I know. He is a Pastor and loves to communicate with people. He is very genuine and very interesting. The second you ask him a question or relate a story to him, he listens completely and looks right at you and asks questions. You know in a second that he is genuinely interested in what you have to say. It means so much and I love him for that.

Imagine you are really excited about a certain event in your life. You are with a friend and wish to relate this event. You start your story and immediately it prompts your friend to think of a similar story in their life. The friend takes over right away to tell you their story. Your story has been ignored, right? When the friend has finished their story, does the friend then ask you about your story? Probably not! The friend is not really interested. Their title could be "It's all about me."

A few years ago, I actually approached a very dear friend who had this habit. It wasn't an easy task; however, in the end, she understood what I was trying to relate to her. Things changed for the good and we are still dear friends. It is so rewarding, when you think of others.

Don't Regret Your Past

Try not to complain about your past. It cannot be changed. Accept it and be happy with your life today. I know that I would change many things from my past. I believe most of us can attest to that. I believe it is a natural feeling to have. I don't want to be an unhappy person because of mistakes I made. They cannot be changed and I believe I did the best I could at the time. Who among us are without errors in our life? We learn as we grow and mature. Try not to have negative feelings. We all may have them and if we don't let them go, we can never appreciate the **now** or the **future** in our lives and the short time we have here on earth.

Growing Older

As we grow older, we start showing our age. I decided long ago to always say "I look so much better now, than I am going to look in years to come." To think this way gives you a sense of feeling good about yourself. Try not to be sad because you may not look as good as you did when you were younger. You will **always** look better today than you are going to look tomorrow. It works for me. I also like this saying, "Do not regret growing older, it is a privilege denied to many." I can definitely relate, since losing my husband at the young age of 44.

My Words to You

My hope is that each of you will be able to relate to my book, both young and old. My wish is that my wisdom will mean something to all of you.

ENJOY THE SUNSET!!

Made in the USA
Lexington, KY
15 June 2011